SO-BKZ-375

Benjamin Franklin couldn't have cooked it if he'd tried. Gertrude Stein preferred roses. Julia Child has other fish to fry. And Harriet Beecher Stowe would have missed the point completely. (After all, this isn't Yankee pot roast!)

The preparation of the Transcendental Boiled Dinner is not so much a gauge of culinary skill as a test of character. John J. Pullen is qualified to make this judgment because in June of 1970 he produced a Boiled Dinner of Transcendental perfection. He has written about his experience in a book that is, in its fanatical solemnity, a comic delight. Mr. Pullen discusses the many contributing factors in this gastronomic and spiritual creation—among them the application of Boyle's Law; the surrounding atmospheric, arboreal and floral conditions (described at their ideal best on the day Mr. Pullen achieved his success); the philosophy of Jonathan Edwards; and the value of concentration and freedom from distraction in the last critical 45 minutes of the boiling, when such mistakes as the dread Turnip Error may be committed.

Cooking the Transcendental Dinner is a scientific, metaphysical and theological exercise. Reading about it is a joyful, refreshing and entertaining experience. You may never accomplish the Transcendental Dinner, but you should at least have the pleasure of knowing what you're missing.

Also by John J. Pullen

PATRIOTISM IN AMERICA (1971)
A SHOWER OF STARS (1966)
THE TWENTIETH MAINE (1957)

THE TRANSCENDENTAL BOILED DINNER

BY JOHN J. PULLEN

J. B. LIPPINCOTT COMPANY

PHILADELPHIA · NEW YORK

Quotations from *Tell Me, Tell Me, Granite, Steel and Other Topics* by Marianne Moore Copyright © 1957, 1958, 1960, 1961, 1962, 1963, 1964, 1965, 1966 by Marianne Moore. All rights reserved. Reprinted by permission of The Viking Press, Inc.

U.S. Library of Congress Cataloging in Publication Data

Pullen, John J
  The transcendental boiled dinner.

  1. Cookery—Anecdotes, facetiae, satire, etc.
2. Cookery, American—New England. I. Title.
PN6231.C624P8   641.8′23   78-37928
ISBN-0-397-00856-2

to the Palmers
including Keith, Apprentice Boilist

THE TRANSCENDENTAL BOILED DINNER

1 ❧ THE NATURE OF TRAN-SCENDENTALISM IN FOOD AND DRINK · · · · · · · ·

MARK TWAIN once remarked that there is nothing so good as Southern corn bread and nothing so bad as a Northern imitation of it.

The same is true, I suspect, of any regional dish that is prepared by strangers far away from its native habitat. Thus, lovers of spoonbread who order it very far north of Richmond, Virginia, or devotees of the baked bean who venture to try it many leagues south of Boston run the risk of severe gastronomical disappointment or even trauma.

I once ordered New England Clam Chowder in a New York City restaurant. It was one of those places given to high ritual in the serving of food—suddenly darkened lights, chimes, flames, ceremonies at tableside and other mummery and flummery which tends to repel one whose Maine background, if not Calvinistic, has at least conditioned him to more frugal expectations, and I should have been warned that something heathenish was to be expected.

Nevertheless, I was not prepared for what followed.

And, indeed, it will hardly be believed when I say that one of a hierarchy of waiters wheeled up a serving wagon and in a chafing dish, over an alcohol fire, began to prepare the proffered New England Clam Chowder with *curry* as one of the ingredients!

The fellow was saved from being instantly throttled only by the obvious fact that he was merely the unknowing and unwitting tool of criminal higher-ups.

However, this is only one of the more bizarre cases of degeneracy in the quality of a regional food when prepared far from its natural environment. Much more to the point are cases in which, on alien territory, diligent and well-meaning people use the proper ingredients and the prescribed method of cookery, and the result is good but not good enough. For some reason the dish does not turn out to be what they hoped for and expected—a food of such ineffable flavor that it has rightly achieved honor and fame by soaring above the mere sense of taste and seeming to slip directly into the soul of the consumer as an ethereal delight.

Something like this also seems to pertain to certain drinks, most particularly to the Martini, which, although it is not regional, seems almost to partake of a special biotic origin.

I for one can immediately recognize and enjoy the indescribable enchantment, more akin to a fragrance than a flavor and somehow irradiating the consciousness with a pale and delicate April-green light, of the Martini that is perfectly prepared. But even though guided by the most scrupulous measurements, I cannot achieve this perfection. Where does the fault lie? In some lack of instinctive understanding of lemon, olive, vermouth and chilled glass? Some slight impatience? Or perhaps a want of Gallic subtlety or Italianate lightness of hand?

I suppose so. However, why is it implied that food or drink of transcendental quality is usually regional?

Henry James once remarked about the works of Hawthorne that "the flower of art blooms only where the soil is deep [and] it takes a great deal of history to produce a little literature." I am persuaded that the same applies to the culinary work of art—therefore that food or drink of surpassing quality has a spirit, style and sensitivity to surroundings to which the character of the maker must be attuned.

What profound consequences must follow upon this assumption!

For several centuries there has been little or no advance in the theory and technique of preparing cookbooks.

Now we see opening up a whole new universe in which psychology, ecology and other disciplines may be brought to bear upon this most essential and widespread form of literature.

It is time that we started moving in that direction, however feeble and halting our first steps may be.

2 ∾ THE TRANSCENDENTAL BOILED DINNER · THE AUTHOR'S RETICENCE IN PUTTING FORWARD HIS IDEAS AND INSTRUCTIONS · A PERSONALITY SCALE AGAINST WHICH THE READER MAY MEASURE HIS PROBABLE COMPETENCE IN PREPARING THE DINNER · · · ·

ECENTLY, having observed in me a peculiar and unaccountable talent for preparing a New England Boiled Dinner—unaccountable because I have no other culinary ability whatever—friends asked me to write down my recipe.

I comply with their request with great diffidence, not only because of my pathetic lack of qualification in general cookery, but because of deep misgivings in putting forward a treatise that may not serve the intended purpose. For while nearly all articles dealing with the preparation of various dishes invariably emphasize how easy the process is, this one must dwell upon very considerable and perhaps insurmountable difficulties.

The chief difficulty arises, I believe, from the specific application of a theory already noted: Success in preparing the New England Boiled Dinner begins with the character of the cook. I do not say that a certain character is admirable. I only say that it is necessary. To give the reader some sort of personality scale against which he can rate himself as likely or not likely to be successful —this by diligent self-examination and comparison of his own traits with those implied—I shall hold up two well-known Americans of the eighteenth century* whose natures stood in such dramatic contrast to each other pertinent to the matter at hand that one can be rated at absolute zero in his probable ability to prepare the Tran-

* Pairs of living Americans might also be used, but as the comparison must be invidious, unnecessary animosity may be avoided by referring the reader to persons of the past upon whose characters (a further advantage) the light of history has shone long enough to reveal their natures rather fully.

scendental Boiled Dinner and the other at, let us say, 10, indicating a superb aptitude for the assignment.

| BENJAMIN | | | | | | JONATHAN | | | | |
| FRANKLIN | | | | | | EDWARDS | | | | |

| 0 | 1 | 2 | 3 | 4 | 5 | 6 | 7 | 8 | 9 | 10 |

As you can see, I would not trust Franklin to boil this Dinner as far as I could throw him. It may be suspected that this is pure prejudice, arising from the fact that Franklin was a deserter from New England who, although born in Boston, went among Philadelphians at an early age. But parochial prejudice is not the reason. Even scrapple does not corrupt or alter character, and it is in this basic requirement that Franklin is found wanting.

Preparation of the Transcendental Boiled Dinner, I now make bold to reveal, is a scientific, metaphysical and theological exercise. On a combination of these counts, Franklin falls short.

True, he was a scientist. But his observations and experiments usually resulted in something merely utilitarian. Examples include a rather inadequate stove which on really cold winter days will not heat a room sufficiently anywhere north of Cos Cob, Connecticut; the lightning rod, in its application a semifraudulent invention which, as promoted by legions of traveling salesmen, was the means of mulcting thousands of hard-working farmers; and bifocals, which, like everything else produced by Franklin, are vastly overrated. He seldom if ever rose above practical inventions into realms of higher sensitivity or thought; consequently, on metaphysics he must be rated as nil.

In his theology, Franklin was loose, vague and timid.*

We will say no more about Franklin, on the basis that it is better to hold up traits to be emulated rather than those to be avoided, and this brings us to the man whose character could not possibly be improved upon as a model for the maker of the Transcendental Boiled Dinner.

Jonathan Edwards, the great New England divine, was not only an acute scientific observer and student— of spider webs, stars, seeds, trees, sound, color, optics, lightning (without foisting a lightning rod on his fellow Americans) and other phenomena—but he went quickly beyond these experiments to the understanding of general laws and unified concepts and, at times, to a seraphic ecstasy in his contemplation of the universe. Thus, he is superb metaphysically in his qualification for the Boiled Dinner assignment. As to his theology, he was an unflinching defender—in an age when increasing sentimentality and muddleheadedness were already beginning to make it unpopular—of the Doctrine of Original Sin, a theory which may be related to the concept that some people just never come up to scratch; they are born on a predestined track to damnation of one kind or another,

* See Franklin's letter of March 9, 1790, to President Ezra Stiles of Yale in which he reveals his weak and liberal religious views and then fearfully adds, "I confide, that you will not expose me to Criticism and censure by publishing any part of this Communication to you."

and there is nothing of any conceivable consequence that can be done about it. (Ah, what wishful, vain and pathetic hopes we entertain that he was not right! Even though the evidence is all around us in small as well as large matters—in the golfer who believes that practice will correct his hook or slice, in the husband who thinks his wife could balance the checkbook if she really tried, in the lady who swears she will take off forty-five pounds, in all those who think that Therapy will help. . . .)

I pause with the realization that the reader may have become considerably puzzled as to why the Doctrine of Original Sin has anything to do with the Boiled Dinner, or why, for that matter, all this talk about science, metaphysics and theology has anything to do with it. It would be vain to attempt an explanation at this point. He must be content to stretch out his hand trustfully and to be led patiently, step by step, along the pathway which leads to understanding.

3 ⮑ A MISNOMER WARNED OF, AND YET RETAINED FOR AESTHETIC REASONS · LIKEWISE, SCIENTIFIC PRINCIPLES INTRODUCED ACCOMPANIED BY INDISPENSABLE CAVEATS · AN EMPIRICAL METHOD INDICATED · · ·

BEFORE going much further, we may as well clear away one possible misunderstanding, which would prove to be a fatal stumbling block if allowed to stand. The New England Boiled Dinner is not boiled. This is one of those false notions that people have about the region, somewhat akin to the idea that the New England Town Meeting is the epitome of participative democracy, when in reality it is only the normal dominion of the interested over the apathetic that prevails everywhere else. The New England Boiled Dinner, properly prepared, is not boiled—boiling will ruin it—the Dinner is *simmered,* because a prime ingredient is beef, and beef should be simmered, not boiled.

However, "New England Simmered Dinner" has a weak, awkward sound and an effeminate sibilance inappropriate to the heartiness of the dish, and so I shall hold to the traditional nomenclature in what follows while abjuring its literal meaning and warning the reader never to forget, even for a second, that boiling must not occur.

Now as to boiling, simmering and so forth, there is a great body of scientific literature* which had a bearing upon the Dinner. The reader may perhaps wish to study some of this himself, beginning appropriately enough with Boyle's Law,† but complete familiarity with it is hardly necessary.

---

* The reader may wish to review the formulae of Dalton, Young, Roche, Biot, Bertrand, Thiesen and Goodenough, especially the last named: $\log p = A - B/T - C \log t - DT + ET^2 + FT^3 + GT^4$.

† Robert Boyle (1627–1691). His law: $PV = $ a constant, at constant temperature (P being the pressure and V the volume of a gas).

I will now mention only a few of the scientific principles involved, more to give the reader a proper respect for the complexities of boiling the Dinner than to lead him to believe that he is thereby gaining very much competence. These are among the most simple of the facts to be remembered:

—*The heat to which a body of water may be raised depends upon its boiling point.*
—*The boiling point depends upon pressure.*
—*Pressure depends on altitude and the general condition of the atmosphere.*
—*The boiling point also may be affected by the presence of dissolved materials.*

However, it would be the grossest of self-deceptions to believe that an understanding or an attempted control of these somewhat mechanical factors will lead to mastery of the Boiled Dinner.

In the first place, what a myriad of influences in Nature, in a changing day, may affect one of them, or all of them, in innumerable permutations and combinations!

And further, although it is granted that these are factors having great determination in the success or failure of the Boiled Dinner, it would be a mistake to assume that there may not be others as well.

The Aquarian nature of the Dinner—the fact that it is cooked in water—may even lead some to believe that it may be worked upon by astrological consequences, and this I wholly reject as a superstition—but I do introduce the thought to underline my belief that this wonderful aqueous dish draws in unto itself aspirates of very mysterious origin extending, I have no doubt, into metaphysical realms.

What we must come to, therefore, is a method of preparing the Dinner which cannot be wholly specific or scientific.

Perfecting the process must involve a series of experiments, or, it would be plainer to say, of dinners, prepared with the most sensitive awareness of all influences and conditions prevailing roundabout, while recording these minutely, so that when perfection is reached, a duplication may later be sought or, as it may happen with some people who are less systematic, a body of perceptions may develop, as they do in learning to play bridge and certain other skills, and operate instinctively.

I will make myself considerably clearer, and the reader will be best served, I believe, if I actually describe in some detail the conditions under which, upon one occasion, Transcendence was achieved.

4 ⟶ THE ENVIRONMENT OF A
TRANSCENDENTAL BOILED DIN-
NER RECORDED WITH SPECIAL
ATTENTION TO WATER AND AIR
· THE NEED FOR QUIET AND
FREEDOM FROM DISTRACTION
NOTED · · · · · · · ·

HE information that follows is placed before the reader not for any direct usefulness it will have to him as a set of directions, but to illustrate the kinds of observations that need to be made and recorded if a successful Boiled Dinner, once attained, is to be repeated. It should be noted and remembered that what works in one environment will probably not work in another. In fact, when the process described in what follows was later repeated some five hundred miles to the south at an altitude close to sea level, the dinner was a failure.

The Dinner that achieved Transcendence was boiled* in an old farmhouse at longitude 67 degrees 49 minutes and 52 seconds west of Greenwich, north latitude 45 degrees 55 minutes and 48 seconds (nearly equidistant from the equator and pole) at an elevation of 615 feet above sea level. By inspection of a map this will be seen to be a point on U.S. Highway No. 1 in Maine.

The farmhouse has been standing at this point for more than a hundred years; it is where I was born. When I was a boy the road ran close to the house and then bent sharply away at a point where there was and still is a deep, perpetually flowing spring, housed in a concrete enclosure. I remember when the road was still horse-traveled and always dusty in summer and when travelers stopped to drink and to water their horses at the spring. It used to be then but is almost never now called the Calais Road (pronounced "Cal'ess" and not "Cal-ay"). When automotive traffic grew, the road was black-topped, but as speed increased, the automobilists had more and more trouble rounding the bend; one, in fact,

* I hope the reader has not forgotten that I do not mean "boiled." I mean "simmered."

hurtled into the spring, which was possibly not too sanitary then because of its closeness to the road.

Then, several years ago, a great blessing and one that rarely occurs nowadays occurred here. A straightening and improvement of U.S. Route 1 placed it not through the living room of the house—which would have been the normal procedure of any truly alert highway department—but farther away from the house, in all a hundred yards or so away, with the state providing an extended driveway to the new road and the old road left as a private footpath for gathering wild flowers and other purposes. Once in a while an old-timer who traveled the Calais Road years ago makes his way in from the new Route 1 and has a dipperful of water at the spring he has always remembered as being so refreshing and so little diminished even by the longest drouth. Then, having had his drink, he may sit there for a while, unable to express what he feels as he gazes at the remnants of the blacktop which winds off into the wild clover, daisies and grasses that have broken their way up through its decaying surface. Perhaps he hears the clopping of horses' hooves and the tympany of Model Ts, and finally he may be able to articulate something like, "A lot of people have gone over that road." It is a ghost road, a little sad.

However, the effect of its abandonment has been to insulate and seclude the farmhouse and the spring, the outlet from which now flows through a channel lined with watercress into a pond. The spring itself is inhabited by a lone trout that eats any bugs falling into the water.

I have dwelt upon this situation because it represents

an instance where "progress" has abated pollution rather than increasing it, and it is in these rather unusual circumstances that the cold, pure water of the old spring is able to contribute so efficaciously to the Boiled Dinner.

Now as to the time when the Boiling took place. It will suffice to say that it was on a day very close to the summer solstice. To give the actual date might be misleading. It is more important to record the exact sort of day it was, which, fortunately, was quite typical of that part of Maine for that time of year and thus provides a set of references that may be exceedingly useful in future attempts to duplicate the Dinner there.

The sun rose at 4:51 A.M., behind a few striated clouds, lying in light layers upon the horizon, the sky above and between them being clear and blue. For a time the clouds were variously colored by the rising sun. Once, for a minute or so, the lower parts of the striae were tinted red while the upper parts remained white, so that with the blue background the eastern sky seemed to be hung with red-white-and-blue bunting.

What could have been more appropriate for the beginning of a day that was to produce the Transcendental Boiled Dinner, that extension and perfection of a dish so deeply rooted in the patriotic traditions of New England!

Having provided this thrilling and prophetic sight, the clouds in the east soon burned away. The blue of the sky grew deeper and more crystalline in its clarity, and the temperature at 9 A.M. stood at about 75 degrees.

Sometimes the air here at this time of morning in late June or early July is, strange as it may seem, reminiscent of Hawaii in its mildness and abundance of floral and arboreal fragrances, although, of course, these are not the same. It is rather the fact that the various scents come so clearly to the nostrils—the smells of new-cut grass, balm of Gilead trees, lilacs, red and white clover blossoms and, if one is walking afield, perhaps the enchanting odor of wild strawberries crushed underfoot.

I make note of this quality of air because it undoubtedly contributes to the Transcendental Boiled Dinner and also because in traveling from the more populated sections of the country up here into this part of Maine it strikes one as more and more remarkable each year, but whether this is a condition of fact or of our own minds, colored by all the talk about environment and pollution, I do not know.

The clearness of the air, and often the quietness, is noticeable in other ways. Riding up here a few days previously, and passing a pile of sawed lumber beside the road, I smelled the resinous odor vividly, even through the window of the rapidly moving car, and one evening while standing on the "old road" at some distance from each other, my Nephew and I were able to conduct a conversation without much effort, although separated by a hundred yards or so. Certain flowers and weeds which are in bloom now—buttercups and orange hawkweed, or devil's paintbrush—shine with almost painful brightness like little suns in an inverted sky of green. I also was able to see, at some distance, a small green-and-yellow frog outgleaming the grass in which it was sitting; it shone as though made of hand-fired porcelain.

Although so clear, still and mild in early morning, the day began to change rapidly, and by the time the dew was drying a thin, milky whiteness had begun to spring up from the horizon. Gradually the whiteness coalesced into wisps of clouds and these in turn grew into lofty towers of cumuli, through the corridors of which the sun, as it passed the zenith, blazed down in shifting waves of light. As the focus of the day turned to the westward, although the rays of the sun were not misted, there was a feeling that the atmosphere was beginning to partake of vapors drawn up by the increasing heat, and it was also moving. This condition continued through the afternoon, and the day, I repeat, was typical of this region of Maine for this time of year: clear and bright in early forenoon, sunny but cloudy in the afternoon.

No instruments were available for measuring pressure and humidity except the barn swallows. These were flying at great heights, which is always an indication that the air is reasonably clear, light and dry and that there will be good weather on the following day as well. When these birds fly nervously and close to the ground, rainy weather is in the offing. Their period of service, however, is limited, because they depart from this latitude of Maine about September 10. I am told that they fly all the way to Mexico, or even to South America, for the winter, which must account for their leaving so early. They go all together and suddenly, before the leaves have begun to turn or there is any other sign of autumn. One morning you get up and after a while you notice that their darting and swooping into and out of the barn, their cheerful chittering and the graceful patterns of their soaring about the sky are all now simply gone, and yet the day may be as hot and summery as one in July. This is a poignant experience that invariably suggests itself as a metaphor of Life, standing for the imperceptibleness of the signals whereby we are all too often warned of the approach of its more melancholy seasons, and recommending to the Boiled Dinner maker, who must be almost prescient in his alertness to signs of approaching trouble, a high degree of awareness and sensitivity.

In continuing our description of the environment in which the Transcendental Boiled Dinner was achieved, we must take note of its narrowest dimensions. This was, of course, the old farmhouse, quite large and airy, but capable of being tightly closed at doors and windows and shielded against sun and weather by overhanging rows of maples on the south and west and on the north partially by a row of cedars, which was once a small ornamental hedge that someone forgot to clip and is now about forty feet in height, contributing a certain spiciness to the air and a shade in which columbines, bluebells and lilies of the valley like to grow.

The house was very quiet; I mention this because it would be (as I shall advance evidence to indicate) impossible to prepare the Transcendental Boiled Dinner in the midst of anything approaching a hubbub, because of the diligent attention and extreme concentration that is called for, particularly in the last hour or forty-five minutes of the process.

This point of freedom from distraction is one which, I fear, the reader will allow to glide too easily into and out of his consciousness, and so I shall seek other opportunities to emphasize its importance later on.

5 ➤ WATER, POT, STOVE, MEAT, SALTING · THE PRELIMINARY BOILING · THE MAIN BOILING · NECESSITY FOR VIGILANCE AGAIN EMPHASIZED · FURTHER SEASONING · VEGETABLES AND THEIR COOKING TIMES · STANDARD, MODIFIED AND ADJUSTED TIMETABLE · MONITORING AND CONTROL · CRITICAL SIZE OF CUT VEGETABLE PARTS · AVOIDANCE OF FRENZY · · · · · · · · ·

IN glancing at this chapter heading and in realizing that he is going to be called upon to absorb, understand and carry out a very considerable number of punctiliously detailed instructions, the aspiring Boiled Dinner maker may very well pause and ask himself, "Oh, well. Really. Is it worth all *that?*" If so, he has come upon a point of self-examination and character that he had better settle—right here and now—before even attempting to go further.

Of course it is worth it—superbly and supremely worth it, but if there is the faintest suspicion that it is not, the aspirant is best advised to turn back and forget the Transcendental Boiled Dinner, for there is a spiritual hedge which he will not be able to jump.

On the other hand, if he is willing to press on, with unquestioning enthusiasm and diligence, let him follow closely this further account of how Transcendence was attained.

The water was drawn from the spring, a distance of 100 feet, by an electric pump through an iron pipe. (It may have been better but it evidently was not essential to go to the spring personally and fetch the water back in a pail or an earthen jug.)

The pot used was made of heavy aluminum. I suspect that an iron pot might have been preferable under certain conditions, which would be (*a*) if one could be found and (*b*) if it could be made perfectly clean and (*c*) if it could be "seasoned" by cooking several ordinary boiled dinners prior to attempting the Transcendental. But years ago, when aluminum utensils first became available, housewives in Maine, and I suppose everywhere else, foolishly threw their iron pots away. Now, even if one can be found, there is the problem of cleaning out rust which has usually pitted the bottom. The merit of the iron pot is that it is somewhat absorptive; therefore, it may be speculated that if one achieved a Transcendental Boiled Dinner in a properly seasoned iron pot, the Ghost or Spirit of the Dinner would lodge in the pores and emerge later, under the influence of heat and simmering, to aid in lifting subsequent Dinners to Transcendence. The dimension thus added to the process, although somewhat spectral, is, I believe, perfectly valid, with a sound basis in the physical properties of iron. With aluminum, one is starting from scratch every time.

The heavy aluminum pot used was five inches deep, with a diameter of nine inches, and a lid. This allows for making a Boiled Dinner for four people, or a Boiled Dinner for two followed by a Hash for two the next day. The pot had a lid which could be clamped on in a way that would achieve the effect of a pressure cooker, but I must hasten to say that it was not so used and that anyone who would subject a Boiled Dinner to a pressure cooker would not only ruin it but should also be personally regarded as a potentially dangerous individual in any relationship or transaction.

A three-and-a-half-pound Beef shin center cut was washed in clear warm water and placed in the pot. Possibly some other cut of unsalted beef would do as well if it has a large marrow bone in it and a little fat. (Many people make their boiled dinner with corned beef, and this practice I am at the moment unable to condemn as a heresy for the very practical reason that those of the corned-beef persuasion may very well be temporarily in the majority, and those of us holding to the unsalted beef still in the role of dissenters, or schismatists. However, let the reader not be deceived by any ecumenicity I display toward corned beef; this will be only for the purpose of quieting the contentious and avoiding interdenominational strife until such time as the forces of truth and enlightenment can effect a reformation.)

To continue, the Beef was covered with the cold spring water, and the water was generously salted.

The stove was a combination wood-gas range using bottled gas. Wood was not used. Purists might insist that the wood fire should be used because that is the way the Puritans cooked the Boiled Dinner, but I think it has certain disadvantages. As will presently be more fully explained, the Dinner must be kept at a simmer and never allowed to boil—or for that matter to cool below a simmer—and this requires an accuracy and quickness of adjustment which is difficult on a wood stove, although an experienced practitioner can accomplish it by shifting the pot to and from the back of the stove, varying the distance from the fire. A more serious disadvantage, perhaps, is that the wood stove heats the atmosphere of the whole room and may affect evaporation from the pot in unpredictable ways.

Let us say this: Probably the greatest of all Transcendental Boiled Dinners, somewhat infused with the slight fragrances of burning maple or yellow birch, would be cooked on a wood stove, but this would require an almost instinctive skill which we no longer possess; the masters of it have been long gone.

As the first step—and this will be referred to hereafter as the Preliminary Boiling—a gas burner was lighted and the water in the pot brought to a strong simmer, at which heat it was allowed to continue for four minutes. Then the pot was taken to the sink, where the meat was removed and put on a plate while the water was poured out and the pot cleaned and rinsed.

Why was the water poured off? And as long as it was going to be poured off, why was it heavily salted?

I must emphasize the impropriety of raising questions such as this. It is vain inquiry into a point of successfully established precedent and doctrine. I can only answer with the supposition that the initial simmering loosens and carries away certain intractable substances on the surface of the meat, bone and marrow. But I cannot pretend to know for certain, because we are dealing, as I hope I have made plain, with matters not entirely susceptible to scientific observation and explanation. The reader must be satisfied and will, I hope, submit himself more trustfully to what follows.

For the second time, the pot was filled with cold spring water. This covered the meat, reaching within about an inch of the top of the pot. There is a difficult judgment involved here, for the meat will be simmering more than three hours before the vegetables are put in, and some of the water will evaporate. If too little evaporates, leaving the pot too full, putting in the vegetables will displace some of the savory broth and cause it to spill out or necessitate a dipping out. If too much evaporates there will not be enough left to cover and cook the vegetables unless water is added, which introduces a weakness. And the rate of evaporation depends on air and weather conditions, which in turn depend on altitude, season of the year and other factors.

1640275

It is even possible that the worst of all disasters will befall your pot—that it will boil dry and scorch the Dinner. Because of a sometimes unpredictable treachery of the weather, this can happen with alarming unexpectedness. One day your Dinner may simmer serenely for hours without your adding a cup of water. Another day you may dance a Devil's jig trying to keep it simmering and not boiling, or simmering and not placid. And on the next day it may suddenly go up in smoke within forty-five minutes, the water having quickly boiled away. Preparing the Transcendental Boiled Dinner is not, therefore, something that you can attend to with a glance now and then. It demands more than four hours of constant vigilance. The lid of the pot, incidentally, should be left off until the very last stages, so that the water may be kept under continuous surveillance to make sure it is simmering, not boiling, and certainly not boiling dry.

To continue with the record: When the second water in the pot was well warmed but before it began to simmer, pepper, two bay leaves and regular and celery salt were added. Again, purists may object to the celery salt, pointing out that two or three stalks of celery may be added and boiled along with the meat. True, this is possible. But I beg to point out a difficulty. Keeping in mind the critical nature of the broth/vegetable ratio that I have been at some pains to explain a few paragraphs previously, it will be understood that when the other vegetables are added it will be necessary to remove the boiled-out celery stalks, which have served their purpose, in order to provide needed space in the pot. My objection to taking out these limp, wilted and unsightly stalks is that it seems to me so distinctly one of the things that a master Boiled Dinner maker just does not do. It is somehow *infra dig.* You may put things into the Boiled Dinner but you do not take things out.

As to how much salt, celery salt and pepper is added: this is a matter for individual taste and judgment.

The meat, after the Main Boiling began, was kept simmering for four hours.

The other ingredients to be added to the Transcendental Boiled Dinner are Turnip, Potato, Cabbage and Carrot.

The times these vegetables take to cook individually in water (allowing a range for different altitudes, atmospheric pressures, boiling points, ages of the vegetables, etc.) I took to be as follows:

Turnip	25–45 minutes
Potato	20–30 minutes
Cabbage	15–20 minutes
Carrot	10–15 minutes

Upon seeing these figures, a lady relative advised me that I was basing my procedure on a partially faulty assumption: that the section of this table pertaining to cabbage and carrot is wrong: that carrots take longer to boil than cabbages: also that there is a much greater range than is indicated here in the boiling time of carrots, from the very young and tender to the very old and tough.

This is the sort of caviling to which the Transcendental Boilist will often be subjected, and, if yielded to, it will lead him into a miasma of doubt. He must dispose of it tactfully, but as quickly as possible. I told the lady what I have already told the reader: that these pages constitute a record of exactly how a Transcendental Dinner was achieved, not a recipe for one. Now if, in that process, assumptions which are somewhat erroneous according to the standards of ordinary mortals figure in the chain of causes and consequences leading to the final result, which is nevertheless glorious, it all the more testifies to the fact that something miraculous has been going on. So to her suggestion that I reverse the positions of the Carrot and Cabbage in the above table, I replied that I dared not do so, and since she persisted in being mystified, I referred her to David Hume's chapter on probabilities in his *Enquiry Concerning Human Understanding* (1748), which has something to say about the complications of cause and effect, and she went away saying she would "look it up sometime."*

The main principle to be observed is that the boiling times of vegetables are different, and if they are all put into the pot at once an impossible situation results, the extremes of which are that they will cook long enough to complete the Turnip—in which case the other vegetables will become mushy—or they will cook long enough to take care of the Carrot only and the other vegetables, save perhaps the Cabbage, will be hard and unedible.

This difficulty is surmounted by selecting an ECT (Elapsed Cooking Time) for each vegetable and com-

* I beg to point out also that the time it takes a vegetable to cook individually may differ somewhat from the time it takes to contribute its essence to the Boiled Dinner, which represents the result of a team effort. The reader will better understand this when that part of Chapter 6 which deals with transubstantiation is reached.

puting a table giving the exact time at which each vegetable is to be inserted. The selection of ECTs is, of course, a matter of experimentation. For reasons which will presently become apparent, the table is called the STANDARD TABLE. In the case of the Transcendental Dinner being described, the following ECTs were selected.

Turnip	44 minutes
Potato	29 minutes
Cabbage	19 minutes
Carrot	14 minutes

Now it will be remembered that the meat must cook four hours. It is within a four-hour period, therefore, that the Standard Table must be constructed. In the case being described, it was decided to start the Main Boiling at 2 P.M. and have the Dinner ready for serving at 6 P.M. This produced the following Standard Table, but please remember that this does not indicate time for the Preliminary Boiling, which was accomplished prior to 2 P.M. and which does not require the precise control that was necessary between 2 and 6 P.M.

STANDARD TABLE

Beef starts simmer	2:00 P.M.
Turnip insertion	5:16 P.M.
Potato insertion	5:31 P.M.
Cabbage insertion	5:41 P.M.
Carrot insertion	5:46 P.M.
Dinner done	6:00 P.M.

These times of vegetable insertion were obtained, as can be seen, by subtracting the ECTs of the various vegetables from the projected finish time of 6 P.M.

However, the process is not quite so simple as this might suggest. The reason is that it is impossible, or nearly so, to manage things so that the meat starts simmering at 2 P.M. exactly. It may start a bit before, or a bit afterward, and these differences must be added to or subtracted from all the entries which follow, producing what is called the MODIFIED TABLE.

To continue with the actual case history, I see by consulting my records that the pot first came to a simmer (in the Main Boiling) at five minutes beyond the hoped-for time of 2 P.M. The tabular picture then was altered to look like this:

		MODIFIED
STANDARD TABLE		TABLE
Beef starts simmer	2:00 P.M.	2:05 P.M.
Turnip insertion	5:16 P.M.	5:21 P.M.
Potato ”	5:31 P.M.	5:36 P.M.
Cabbage ”	5:41 P.M.	5:46 P.M.
Carrot ”	5:46 P.M.	5:51 P.M.
Dinner done	6:00 P.M.	6:05 P.M.

Yet, since we are speaking in terms of the utmost precision, there is still another segment of our calculation to be entered, and this is the ADJUSTED TABLE. This is usually necessary for the following reason: When the cold vegetable is inserted, the water is momentarily cooled below the point where simmering ceases. If this hiatus lasts longer than a minute, its time must be added to this and each subsequent entry on the schedule. For example, in the case related, Potato insertion caused loss of simmer of one minute, requiring the following adjustment:

STANDARD TABLE		MODIFIED TABLE	ADJUSTED TABLE
Beef starts simmer	2:00 P.M.	2:05 P.M.	
Turnip insertion	5:16 P.M.	5:21 P.M.	
Potato "	5:31 P.M.	5:36 P.M.	5:37 P.M.
Cabbage "	5:41 P.M.	5:46 P.M.	5:47 P.M.
Carrot "	5:46 P.M.	5:51 P.M.	5:52 P.M.
Dinner done	6:00 P.M.	6:05 P.M.	6:06 P.M.

And, of course, had there been a loss of simmer of more than a minute during both Cabbage and Carrot insertions, the table would have had to be extended even farther to the right under two additional Adjusted segments.

There is an alternate way of accomplishing the desired result without recourse to the mathematical adjustments as follows: Just before putting in the cold vegetables, bring the broth to a *boil*,* then quickly pop in the vegetable, and when the boiling consequently disappears and the surface of the broth becomes placid, turn the burner still higher until a simmer is restored—then quickly turn it down again before boiling ensues, and adjust to a steady simmer. If accomplished in less than a minute (the essential requirement), this procedure will call for a nicety of judgment and dexterity of hand

* This time I do mean *boil*.

not involved in the more precise mathematical method—also for a certain recklessness of spirit which I am not altogether sure should be among the desiderata of the Transcendental Boiled Dinner maker's character. Nevertheless, I do not rule it out.

There is one other important consideration having to do with the vegetables. They must be properly cut up. Pieces cut too small will cook too fast and disintegrate so that a soup or stew, not a Boiled Dinner, results. Pieces cut too large will not cook long enough. Thus, in improper cutting, the whole purpose of the precise timetable may be frustrated.

In the case recorded the Turnip was cut into eighths. The Potato was cut into pieces not above two inches thick. The Cabbage was cut into eighths. And the Carrot into halves, lengthwise.

As to the amount of vegetables to be added, it is as much as may be crammed into the pot (and following Carrot insertion it will be advisable to put the lid on so as to prevent spillage). As to the proportions, the shares of vegetables by volume should be equal, and this involves an extremely critical estimate. One very common mistake is the Turnip Error. Since the Turnip is the first vegetable to be inserted, it is easy to put in too much; this will mean that you can put in less Potato, Cabbage and Carrot—or less of one of them—and this will spoil the delicate balance of constituents which is essential to Transcendence, replacing their indescribably delicious harmony with a turnipy discord.

Proportion, then, as in all art, is something that must be precisely controlled.

It is important to have the vegetables peeled and

cut up well ahead of times of insertion. They can be placed in pans of cold water to keep them fresh. They must all be ready, and readily at hand, because in the last forty-five minutes of cooking, beginning with Turnip insertion, there is no time to peel or cut; in fact, there is very little time in which to think; often split-second decisions must be made and rapid adjustments accomplished in order to hold to the required degree of precision. And there is no worse sight than the Boiled Dinner maker who, pressed into a frenzy, loses his wits and sees the whole venture collapse after having put in nearly four hours of work.

It is here that I must warn of a specific danger. At this stage of making the Dinner, when tension has been building up for more than three hours and when there is a natural tendency to seek relief, the idea of having the predinner cocktail may suggest itself. Here I must speculate—although I do not suggest it as an invariable or even a frequent condition—that those capable of preparing a really supernal Boiled Dinner may include a few persons who have a weakness long attributed to certain great geniuses (I think of Edgar Allen Poe) who, in reaching toward perfection, encounter a point beyond which their elevated concepts of Art cannot go and who therefore reach for the bottle.

This tendency, from whatever motive it arises, must be resisted, especially in the last forty-five minutes, when the pace of time seems to pick up like that of a jet upon takeoff and when certain judgments must be made and adjustments managed within fractions of seconds. In this situation, the Boiled Dinner maker should not risk dulling the edge of his perceptions with alcohol. Let him, when his triumph is achieved and the Dinner is upon the platter, sink down into an easy chair and enjoy his Martini or Manhattan (if he can resist for a few moments the almost maniacal appetite which the sight and smell of the Boiled Dinner arouse). But while the Boiled Dinner is under preparation let him think of a cocktail no longer than he would consider downing a pint of Old Crow before starting down the New Jersey Turnpike behind the wheel of a powerful motorcar.

6 ⤙ A PAUSE TO BRING SCIEN-
TIFIC AND METAPHYSICAL CON-
SIDERATIONS INTO BALANCE ·
JONATHAN   EDWARDS   AGAIN
HELD UP AS MODEL · HARMONY
OF INGREDIENTS PRAISED · THE
TRANSCENDENTAL BOILED DIN-
NER   EATEN   ·   ITS   THEOLOGY
DWELT UPON ·   ·   ·   ·   ·   ·

AFTER dwelling so long on precise method, I must stop and remind myself that I do not wish to delude the reader into believing that the Transcendental Boiled Dinner is reducible to any easily computed formula, or that I have placed that delectable dish within his grasp by these simple directions.

Indeed, I am willing to admit that the Transcendental deliciousness achieved on the June day described with the methods reported may have been partly an accident—that some mysterious, unobserved influence may also have been at work. It is certain as can be that the same process, had it been repeated beside a large body of water such as the ocean, or in the deserts of Arabia, or in southern France with a mistral blowing, would have failed. Could there not have been far less dramatic influences which affected the outcome of the success in Maine? Did a passing bank of clouds, unnoticed, chill the air for a critical length of time? Was there a minute or two of more intense than usual cosmic rays? Did the wind swing around and blow from the direction of the Bay of Fundy right after Cabbage insertion?

The reader will perhaps begin to understand now why Jonathan Edwards represents the mind which seems best able to cope with the Boiled Dinner on both scientific and mystic counts. In one of his works, "Things to Be Considered," alongside his mathematical demonstrations, will be found passages such as this:

To show how the Motion, Rest, and Direction of the Least Atom *has an influence on the motion, rest and direction of every body in the Universe; and to show*

how, by that means, every thing which happens, with
respect to motes, or straws and such little things, may be
for some great uses in the whole course of things,
throughout Eternity; and to show how the least wrong
step in a note, may, in Eternity, subvert the order of the
Universe; and to take note of the great wisdom that is
necessary, in order thus to dispose every atom at first, as
that they should go for the best . . .

If there is anyone other than Jonathan Edwards whose universal awareness and cast of thought is more worthy of emulation than his in striving for the Transcendental Boiled Dinner, his name does not come to mind. If you seek this prize, strive to be like him!

The harmony which Edwards so often speaks of is superbly illustrated by the vegetables in the Boiled Dinner: Turnip, Potato, Cabbage and Carrot. They have qualities that blend, with the other ingredients, in a heavenly flavor. Thus, the Carrot is a sweet, pious vegetable—the Potato also inclined toward sweetness—but both are somewhat wanting in zest. This is made up for by the Cabbage and the Turnip, which, wholesome and dutiful as they are, nevertheless contribute spiciness and pungency. The savoriness of the meat, bone and marrow adds hearty gusto. Through and among all these ingredients the salted and peppered beef broth, slightly enlivened with bay and celery, and bearing tiny jewels of hot fat, circulates and penetrates, effecting a blending of all flavors, in fact, a transubstantiation of elements.

To return to the Boiled Dinner I have been describing: As it neared its climax shortly after 6 P.M., what an entrancing aroma filled the kitchen of the old farmhouse! The sun had descended to a point where it was shining into the western windows through the trees, irradiating the leaves with greenish gold, and for a moment the illusion prevailed that the sunlight and the gorgeous aroma were one—also that there had been a mystical blending of the day, the hour, the June foliage, Nature herself, into the contents of the pot! Also noted were certain human reactions in a young Nephew who was allowed into the kitchen at this point: eyes taking on a staring look, pinpoints of light deep in the pupils, lips opened slightly, the nostrils flared, a quickened breathing.

When the contents of the pot were placed on a large platter, it was seen that very little broth was left in liquid form. It had nearly all been absorbed into the solid substances, leaving only enough to have prevented the Dinner from burning. (This, I suppose, was among the several niceties, almost beyond calculation, which had brought the Dinner to perfection.)

Two people, the Nephew and I, sat down to the table. Such is the mouth-watering allure of a Transcendental Boiled Dinner that if only one person were present and no social amenities were required, it probably would not be eaten, it would be ravened upon. In this case, excesses of appetite were restrained. But even so, half of the tremendous platter of Boiled Dinner disappeared! And next day the other half, reheated, vanished as quickly. (The Transcendental Boiled Dinner may be reheated in a double boiler with very little loss of flavor, or it may be made into a rapturous Hash.)

One probable reaction should be noted. When the

Dinner is first displayed on the platter, it may be believed by some that the meat has cooked down to too small a portion. But this will be found to be immaterial, for in its Transcendescence, there is now in the Dinner no such thing as Beef, Turnip, Potato, Cabbage and Carrot. The meat has instilled its flavor into the vegetables, and they theirs into it, all in one unified deliciousness, so that a bite of any one part of the Dinner is no less in flavor than any other part. Yet it is not a soup or a stew. Each component is preserved in its own form and shape!

What we have in this congregation is what Jonathan Edwards described in his "Notes on the Mind," when he spoke of a thing being pleasant to the mind because it is a "shadow of love" and said that "when one thing sweetly harmonizes with another, as the Notes in musick, the notes are so conformed, and have such proportion to one another, that they seem to have respect one to another, as if they loved one another."

So it is with the constituents of the Transcendental Boiled Dinner.

Nothing should be allowed to disrupt their empyrean harmony.

I think it wise and essential to point out that the reader, should he assay the Dinner, will be almost certainly tempted to put in other ingredients. I do not wish to take up and dismiss in turn all the different vegetables which will propose themselves to the mind, and, indeed, some of them hardly need comment.

It must be apparent, for example, that adding the tomato—which is so susceptible to mushiness and to dissolution into seediness—would be an abomination in the sight of Heaven, and I say this as one who loves the tomato—in its proper place.

Nor should it be necessary to publicly proscribe the violent horseradish.

The beet, sweet and endearing though it is, does not belong in the Boiled Dinner because it is a Bleeding Heart which, if nicked or wounded ever so slightly, would color everything with its sentimental effusion. I would have no objection to having a platter of buttered beets on the table when the Boiled Dinner is served, but they must be cooked separately and not even thought of as part of the Dinner proper.

The parsnip may also suggest itself as a candidate, but it would be too strong and vigorous a participant— one likely to overcome the others and exert a dominance which would upset the final delicate flavor. Of it, I shall say very simply that a vegetable which can be left in the ground all through a Maine winter, surviving the frosts and freezes and emerging in the spring as sprightly and spicily sweet as ever, is a vegetable to be reckoned with, and the place to reckon with it is not in the Transcendental Boiled Dinner.

But I am afraid that I am beginning to do the reader a disservice when I imply, through the merely rational discussion pro and con of these vegetables, that he really has the right of consideration, comparison, evaluation and rejection or acceptance of ingredients when it comes to the Transcendental Boiled Dinner. This is where we need, again, to attune ourselves with Jonathan Edwards and with theology.

If it is asked how this applies to the Boiled Dinner, may I suggest that a moment's thought and reflection will suffice to clarify the historical role of theology, which has been mainly to stop people from doing things, close something down, shut somebody out and the like. It has been largely repressive, restrictive and exclusive. Do I condemn this? No! For how otherwise would a theology keep the wolf confined to his thicket and its flock from wandering into alien fields, away from Paradise? How otherwise would it deserve the single-minded devotion which, by definition, is religion? How otherwise be more than a vaporous philosophy?

In that light, when we consider what should be kept out of the Transcendental Boiled Dinner, I will say and I will repeat as long as I am asked, that *everything* should be kept out except what I have told you should be put in.

This is the Only True Boiled Dinner.

I am aware that I will now be accused of INTOLERANCE!—a charge which is so often leveled at proponents of other nonsecular disciplines—but I point out that this word in today's usage has unjustly come to be considered reprehensible *per se;* once this dreadful word is applied to an individual, few people even stop to consider the relative merits or demerits of whatever it is the accused person is accused of being intolerant *of.*

Far from having too much intolerance, we have too little! For if we are to have craftsmanship, we must be intolerant of bungling. If we are to have learning, we must be intolerant of ignorance. If we are to have beauty and poetry, we must be intolerant of vulgarity. If we are to have excellence in anything, we must be intolerant of nonexcellence.

This, too, must be the spirit of the Boiled Dinner,

but since I fear the reader will believe I have begun to engage in needless ranting, I will defer discussion of this point of doctrine (the theological necessity of exclusion) until subsequent pages, when its validity will perhaps have become more apparent.

7 ⮑ POTENTIALITIES OF WOM-
EN AS BOILERS OF THE DINNER
CONSIDERED · EIGHTEEN AP-
PRAISED, BEGINNING WITH MARI-
ANNE MOORE AND CONCLUDING
WITH RIMA, THE JUNGLE GIRL ·
WORKINGS OF THE HAND OF
PROVIDENCE DISCERNED · AN AS-
TOUNDING REVELATION WITH
RESPECT TO WOMEN VIS-À-VIS
THE DINNER · · · · · ·

WE now come to that part of the disquisition where it is necessary for the author to tread with the greatest care, for it is here that he exposes himself not only to the damning (in the current view) charge of INTOLERANCE! but also to the still more damning (because it is the more specific) indictment of DISCRIMINATION!

It is in this chapter that we must deal with women in relation to the Transcendental Boiled Dinner. Since an unswerving pursuit of and regard for the truth is the very essence of dealing with the Dinner, I must say, however reluctantly, that women, as a class of people, generally, are not outstandingly competent to prepare it.

Now let me very hastily add the belief that women are eminently qualified to make transcendental other things. Also that there may even be a few women who are capable of making the Transcendental Boiled Dinner.

But on the whole their traits, qualities and characteristics simply do not combine and converge to achieve an apex of excellence *in this particular endeavor.*

Many women cannot boil the Transcendental Dinner for the same reason that they cannot play chess: The required degree of planning and forethought is abhorrent to them.

Most women, however, fail under larger considerations: They do not embody that combination of scientific, metaphysical and theological aptitudes which is essential to perfection. This can probably be best illustrated by returning to the character-personality scale against which, at the beginning of this work, the reader was given an opportunity to measure himself as to his being a potential boiler of the Transcendental Dinner.

BENJAMIN   JONATHAN
FRANKLIN   EDWARDS

0   1   2   3   4   5   6   7   8   9   10

It is possible to think of a great many ladies—particularly rather elderly ones—who resemble Benjamin Franklin not only in appearance but in habit of thought.

But where today, or where by leafing through all the pages of history, do we find a female Jonathan Edwards, that paragon of excellence in all three realms: science, metaphysics and theology?

As Artemus Ward said, answering a question as to where the equal of George Washington could be found "no whares, or eny whare else."

However, I do still think there may be, or may have been, a few women who, without having any actual top reference point on our scale, we might place at 7 or even 8 as possibly successful boilers of the Dinner, even though in actuality these may never have attempted one.

By reference to her poetry and certain facts that were known about her I would, for example, look favorably upon the name of the late Marianne Moore. Since her record reveals no clear-cut or obvious qualifications related to the Dinner, it is necessary to draw conclusions from significant clues, beginning with her preoccupation with baseball.

Baseball is the most scientific of sports, a game of almost astronomical niceties and precisions—of time-and-space relationships resulting in decisions that are always trembling in the balance. For instance, the distance to first base is just such that a grounder will necessitate the utmost exertion on the part of both fielder and runner to decide the contest at first, while in a double play a tenth of a second may mean the difference between success and failure. Also, there is a way in which baseball resembles the universe itself, in which, as I believe Sir James Jeans once remarked, there is much of pattern and form but almost nothing of substance. Likewise, baseball is primarily nothingness. Mostly, nothing is happening on the field. A time-and-motion study would, I have no doubt, show that action occurs only about 0.5 percent of the time and that baseball is 99.5 percent talk.

So here is a sport that is both extremely scientific and highly metaphysical, and it is hard to believe that Marianne Moore could be recorded as so great an appreciator of the game without also believing that scientific and metaphysical qualities of mind were born in her.

More evidence of all this is found in one of her books, *Tell Me, Tell Me*. In speaking of poetic writing, Miss Moore says on one of its pages, "Wariness is essential where an inaccurate word could give an impression more exact than could be given by a verifiably accurate term." What an insight this provides as to her probable talent for preparing the Boiled Dinner! Indeed, how applicable it is to the Dinner itself, which is described by an inaccurate word, boiled!

Then, in one of her poems in this book she uses the phrase "metaphysical newmown hay." When someone asked her what *that* meant, she replied, "Oh, something like a sudden whiff of fragrance in contrast with the doggedly continuous opposition to spontaneous conversation that had gone before."

That is the very essence of the Boiled Dinner; a sudden whiff of fragrance in contrast with the doggedly continuous opposition of many factors, through which it finally wafts its way like the sweet breath of a new-mown field of clover.

I believe, too, that there are many women who prepare foods, other than the Boiled Dinner, of transcendental quality, and I have in mind my second cousin Carrie, who, come to think of it, resembles photographs I have seen of Marianne Moore.

Carrie makes what she calls Seven-Day Pickles. The name derives from the fact that it takes seven days to make these pickles, an expenditure of time that, corresponding to the cycle of Creation in Genesis, signifies that something remarkable is going forward.*

And indeed, it is. One who tastes a Seven-Day Pickle floats for several seconds in a little cloud of entrancing deliciousness. Even as I write this I can feel their flavor impinging delightfully upon my palate, with a slight, spicy piquancy rising into my lower nasal passages—so that I catch a quick, evanescent, but actual taste of the Seven-Day Pickles! And this is the highest test of the transcendental food—its ability to conjure itself up from the flavor cells of the mind's memory bank. Or can it be extrasensory perception?

And yet—this is the whole point—does Carrie fully realize all this? For it may possibly be argued that if a

* Also involved is an operation analogous to the rotation of the earth. The gallon glass jar containing the pickles during the seven-day period is turned upside down repeatedly so that the salt, spices and other solids will not settle but pass frequently down through the cucumber slices, caressing them with a constant infusion of flavor.

food is truly transcendental it must involve the maker as well as the taster in a significant Experience, including a heightened awareness of the surroundings and their effect upon the preparation of food, the origin of the ingredients and other factors, not the least of which may possibly be a great deal of conversation. To the contrary, there is no fuss connected with Carrie's Seven-Day Pickles. She just goes ahead and makes them. And were she to record for your guidance how she makes them, it would all be written down in a hundred words or less: do this, do that, do this and do that. One is compelled to recognize a Pickle of a quality indicating transcendental competence in the preparer but is puzzled by the absence of treatise or dissertation.

In seeking the names of other possible boilers of the Dinner in addition to Marianne Moore and Carrie, I have conducted an intensive survey of history, legend, literature, current events, the arts and in general the whole record of womankind. I regret to say that with a few exceptions the results have been meager or uncertain. Nevertheless, the reader may be interested in the reasons why some women have been rejected while others have been accepted or tentatively approved as worthy of further investigation.

As in the case of Marianne Moore, the criteria are somewhat vague and intuitive. They can be taken to resemble only a sort of luminous mist, such as might be created by a mass of minute particles in interstellar space; and, as it may be imagined, through this screening opacity various noted women appear either brightly or dimly, as do the stars, or appear and then disappear. Those who shine most strongly and constantly are ladies who had or have remarkable, often abstruse powers, or phenomenal influences, or talents that transcended the situations in which life placed them.

The finalists included Helen of Troy, Harriet Beecher Stowe (there is no attempt at chronology or any other system here), The Loathly Lady, Margaret Fuller, Anne Bradstreet, Emily Dickinson, Marie Taglioni, Minna Marx, Harlean Carpenter, Elissa Landi, Sophia Loren, Gertrude Stein, Julia Child, Valentina V. Tereshkova, the Blessed Damozel and Rima, the Jungle Girl.

Possibly some of these come to the reader's attention as a surprise, and I must admit to having had the same reaction when certain names first swam into view. For example, I had not thought of Elissa Landi for years. And yet suddenly there she was! Nor had Marie Taglioni been very much in mind. In fact, I have had to freshen my memory on some of these people, and it may serve the reader to the same purpose if I quickly run through the list with appropriate comments.

First, there is Helen of Troy, and Marlowe's famous apostrophe comes immediately to mind:

Was this the face that launched a thousand ships
And burnt the topless towers of Ilium?

However much this might indicate supernormal powers, considering Helen's general inattentiveness to domestic responsibilities it must be feared that she would have burnt the Boiled Dinner as well. She is disapproved. We encounter a similar difficulty with respect to Harriet Beecher Stowe, who through her *Uncle Tom's Cabin* was partly responsible for starting another big war. According to my information, Mrs. Stowe was a simply terrible cook; her cakes and pies are said to have been almost indigestible, and this represents a failing too fundamental to overlook.

The Loathly Lady is a stock figure in old romances, a female counterpart to Beast in *Beauty and the Beast,* who is hideous (the effect of a spell that has been cast upon her), but when she finds a husband the enchantment ceases, her ugliness disappears and she becomes stunningly beautiful. As is well known, many of these old legends have a basis in facts, but the facts sometimes get reversed as the tale passes from one generation of tellers to another. Extensive research has led me to advance as plausible the theory that the enchantment did not cease at marriage—it began. In other words, the Lady continued to be as homely as ever, but her ability to make the Transcendental Boiled Dinner or something very much like it cast a spell over her husband, to whom ever afterward she seemed a creature of surpassing loveliness.

Margaret Fuller must be admitted to consideration if for no other reason than that she is clearly labeled as a Transcendentalist—one of the so-named group that included Emerson, Thoreau and Hawthorne. However, I find nothing in the record to indicate that Margaret ever reached the heights of Transcendentalism that is represented by the Dinner; the reason, I think, is found in a memoir left by her friend Thomas W. Higginson, in which it is strongly hinted that the poor woman had indigestion, and while the Dinner itself is one of the easiest of foods to assimilate, this unfortunate condition must have left her imperfectly attuned to its finer aspects. This is a matter for regret, for had Margaret Fuller been in possession of this rare talent, she would have been—with her unflinching determination in promoting objects of her interest—an unparalleled gospeler of the Dinner.

The reader will begin to suspect that I have searched very diligently but with increasing disappointment among the women of New England for one who would seem to have qualified as a Transcendental Boilist. Such is indeed the case. For example, Anne Bradstreet (1612?–1672), member of the Massachusetts Bay Colony, author of the first original poetry to be written in New England, a devout Puritan and appreciator of Nature, may seem to have been perfect for the assignment, but although her credentials are impeccable, we are given pause by the realization that her verses were not, and I must say I find her candidacy very unlikely. Even if so much credit is due her for her contributions to American poesy, one would hesitate to entrust the Dinner to a quality of craftsmanship that had still so far to evolve.

So often, it seems, these basic kinds of difficulty are encountered in the New England part of the survey: Margaret Fuller's having indigestion, and Mrs. Stowe's causing it, and Anne Bradstreet's falling short. And yet when we come to Emily Dickinson, another descendant of the earliest Puritans in America, how glowingly rewarded is our search! Consider her magnificent disregard of the world outside her own sphere—her writing of hundreds and hundreds of dazzling poems, not caring at all that only three or four would be published in her lifetime! Consider the mystic, illusive quality of her verses, and notice how perceptively so many of them deal with winds, sun, sky, rain and other aspects of a passing day. She speaks, for example, of the sun taking a yellow whip and driving the fog away . . . of a sea of summer air washing around the house . . . of a cloud's "surprising" the sky and so forth. How observant she would have been of atmospheric conditions so important to the Dinner! And how impervious to distractions in her kitchen! As a potential Boilist of the highest order, Emily Dickinson is looked upon by the author with an enthusiasm equaled only by that which is inspired by Marianne Moore.

Marie Taglioni, the Italian-Swedish dancer of the nineteenth century whose lightness and ethereality are legendary, is pointed to as exemplary of a class that is worthy of further investigation: ballet dancers. It seems to me that they would move with a particular precision and grace through the complicated pattern that begins with Turnip insertion. Likewise, I wish that I had more information on Minna Marx, who will be recalled as the mother not of Karl but of Groucho and the other Marx Brothers. The daughter of a German magician, she had much to do with taking her sons away from whatever inconsequential things they were doing in early life and launching them upon a transcendental career. Harlean Carpenter (Jean Harlow) and Elissa Landi represented talent that far transcended the packages in which Hollywood placed them. So, today, does Sophia Loren, who in the opinion of the Author of this work* could boil the Dinner or do anything else.

* And of the Editor.

It is upon the name of Gertrude Stein that I have paused for the longest time and with the greatest indecision. I must say that I regard with considerable doubt her long residence in Paris, but I do not wish to harm international relations by elaborating too far—they are bad enough now—so let me simply remind the reader that Franklin lived for a time in and had a great affinity for that city (where some of his activities, I understand, were scandalous), and also that the French assiduously stirred up the Indians against us here in New England. Without my pursuing the matter further and more explicitly, I think that why the French influence in cookery —respected though it is—simply is not compatible with the New England Boiled Dinner will be sufficiently grasped. In fact, were Auguste Escoffier himself to attempt it, the result would not be satisfactory; it might be delicious, but it would not be the Dinner.

On the more favorable side, it still must be recognized that Gertrude Stein's home at 27 rue de Fleurus was for many years a center of encouragement to the arts, which indicates that she might have appreciated so great an art as that of preparing the Boiled Dinner. What we finally are forced to come down to is consideration of her own writing. Did it, in fact, signify the transcendental ability or was it merely, as Mencken once put it, a lot of "tosh"? I had been pondering upon this question several days when suddenly the key to it appeared in the September 25, 1971, issue of *Saturday Review*. It was a letter from George Seldes referring to a previous article in SR in which, he said, Gertrude Stein had been slightly misquoted: she had actually written "Rose is a rose is a rose"—not "A rose is a . . ."

and so on. And further, she had once told his brother Gilbert that Rose was a person, not a flower, and this, said George Seldes, "totally changes the meaning."

Totally changes it, perhaps, but makes it no clearer. And this, of course, is highly significant; it is one of the signs of a truly transcendental work that any attempt to explain it only removes it to another plane of incomprehension.* So the answer hinged upon two questions: (a) Was Gertrude Stein serious in what she wrote? and (b) Was George Seldes serious in what *he* wrote? If the answer to both questions was yes, then there was a possibility that Gertrude Stein might have qualified as a Transcendental Boilist. But of course she could not be queried at this late date, and that left only Mr. Seldes.

Remembering that I had one of Mr. Seldes' books, I rushed to the bookshelves, found the volume and gazed long and earnestly at the portrait and the brief biography of the author on the jacket. He had been born, it said, in New Jersey but was at the time of the publication of the book (1953) living in Connecticut, and I noted that the letter to *Saturday Review* had been written from Vermont. This meant that he was moving farther and farther into New England and so made his statement worthy of increasing respect. But had he been serious in the letter to SR? I studied his portrait for any telltale signs of chronic levity but found it enigmatic. I thought of telephoning Mr. Seldes, but then it dawned upon me that such a call was impossible, for he could only re-

---

* I am perfectly aware of the implications that exist in this statement, but I do hope the reader has not gone all the way through these pages under the impression that what I am doing is *explaining* the Dinner.

spond to it in one of two ways: with amused contempt or by treating it as an impertinence.

The status of Gertrude Stein with respect to the Dinner must therefore be left in suspension.

The name of Julia Child, the cooking instructress of TV fame, has been presented to me, and my conclusion is that she might succeed with the Dinner, so capable does she seem (and in spite of the French influence evident in her program), but success would require a radical change in personality, and I don't know whether that is possible. Her whole attitude, at least as projected on television, is one of hearty assurance and exuberant good cheer. With Julia it is zip, slap, bang— and look! nothing to it. And of course the Boiled Dinner cannot be approached in this frame of mind; the boiler's manner must inevitably be one of nervousness and doubt, for he knows very well that he may not bring it off, and the apprehensive alertness that this attitude fosters is, in fact, essential to reaching Transcendence.

Little doubt attends the name of Valentina V. Tereshkova, the Russian and first woman astronaut who parachuted to earth in June, 1963, after having made forty-eight orbits of the globe in a spacecraft. The fact that she managed an enterprise in which so many things might have gone wrong but none did, and the certainty that she would conduct herself with superb coolness and efficiency in the critical last forty-five minutes of preparing the Dinner (which, indeed, very much resembles the descent of astronauts to earth in the tension engendered) leads one to believe wholeheartedly in Valentina's qualification.

I have saved until near the last the candidate whose

performance I contemplate with the greatest pleasure: the Blessed Damozel who, Rossetti tells us, "leaned out/ From the gold bar of Heaven" and whom he portrays as a character of the greatest beauty and nobility.

I can envision the Transcendental Boiled Dinner, as prepared by the Damozel, being borne in to the dining place upon a great cumulus sort of cloud, tinted by some inner effulgence with rays of sublime colors (my preference would be light pink and gold), accompanied by flights of cherubim and seraphim and by the peals of trumpeters and the silvery notes of harpists. It is possible, of course, that at that altitude ("So high, that looking downward thence/ She scarce could see the sun") the Damozel might encounter unusual problems of pressure and evaporation, but from all Rossetti tells us of her, I am positive she could have overcome them.

It is from this high plane, however, that we must descend rather rudely to earth and there ruefully reckon how small have been our gleanings among the women of history, legend, literature and art, and realistically recognize how unessential a competence in preparing the Boiled Dinner is in the life of Woman. This was brought home to me when I reread W. H. Hudson's *Green Mansions*, thinking of Rima, the ethereal forest girl who is described with the use of so many words like "iridescent glory" . . . "fairylike loveliness" . . . "changeful splendor" and other terms indicating a diaphanous, possibly a transcendent quality. But I stopped after this passage:

> *She moved quickly away to the fire, and presently returned with an earthenware dish of roasted pumpkin*

and sweet potatoes, and kneeling at my side fed me
deftly with a small wooden spoon. I did not feel grieved
at the absence of meat and the stinging condiments the
Indians love, nor did I even remark that there was no
salt in the vegetables, so much was I taken up with
watching her beautiful delicate face while she minis-
tered to me. The exquisite fragrance of her breath was
more to me than the most delicious viands could have
been; and it was a delight each time she raised the spoon
to my mouth to catch a momentary glimpse of her eyes,
which now looked dark as wine when we lift the glass to
see the ruby gleam of light within the purple.

We do not need to go any further with *that*. It is
plain that the dinner was no good, and that there was
no reason for it to be any good; the narrator wouldn't
have had the slightest idea of what he was eating any-
way. And this incident, I think, is symbolic. It provides
us with one of those little touches of insight that literature often supplies where life cannot. It reminds us that
the realm and rule of women is one of allurement and
artifice and is certainly not to be found in that triad of
disciplines so essential to the preparation of the Dinner:
science, metaphysics and theology.

Nevertheless, as we continue along this avenue of
thought, we find that a paradox is lurking nearby.
Women, it is said, are impractical and illogical. Yet in
contradistinction to this belief, and as thousands of cookbooks written by or for them in severe and staccato
informational style will testify, their attitude toward
cooking is characterized by a solid matter-of-factness.

I have tried on several occasions in conversing with lady friends and relatives to enlarge their understanding and convey to them some comprehension of the Boiled Dinner in its full, Transcendental dimensions. But just when I am at my most eloquent and therefore, it should be thought, am the most convincing, their eyes take on a glassy, vacant stare and they begin to fidget and to edge nervously away.

The full significance of this behavior did not dawn upon me until one day when, in a moment of relaxation, I was idly reading that gem of metaphysical literature by George Berkeley published in 1713 and entitled *Three Dialogues Between Hylas and Philonous, The Design of Which Is Plainly to Demonstrate the Reality and Perfection of Human Knowledge, the Incorporeal Nature of the Soul and the Immediate Providence of a Deity in Opposition to Sceptics and Atheists.*

Throughout these dialogues Philonous scores against Hylas, who is what I believe would now be called a straight man, a long series of points in support of Berkeley's well-known belief in the nonexistence of matter. In the course of one exchange he says to Hylas, "And, nothing could be plainer than that divers persons perceive different tastes in the same food; since that which one man delights in, another abhors. And how could this be, if the taste were something really inherent in the food?"

Upon reading this there came to me, in a tremendous flash of mental illumination, the realization of just what women's trouble with the Dinner is. Theirs is a Berkeleian difficulty.

To them there is no such thing as a Transcendental Boiled Dinner!

It simply does not exist!

In one of my last conversations with a lady on the subject of the Dinner it occurred to me (perhaps a bit too late as it happened) that I might lead her toward the Truth if I spoke to her very earnestly and urged her to read Berkeley, so that she might begin by understanding the nature of her own intellectual problem. But by the time we had reached that point in the rather extended conversation she had backed away toward her motorcar, which was standing in the driveway—had receded, in fact, to such a considerable distance that I am not sure she was able to hear what I was calling to her; and, in fact, the title of the work, especially if one is trying to refer someone to the First Dialogue as distinct from the Second or Third, is an extremely difficult thing to shout, not to say a somewhat embarrassing one if there are other people about. However, just before she rather hastily entered the car and drove away, I thought she did agree to do the suggested reading sometime (I believe it is this I understood her to say) "when I am at the public library."

I suppose it is fortunate that the ability to make the Boiled Dinner is, apparently, denied to most women.

If it were otherwise, what a weapon would be added to their arsenal of blandishments and enticements!

What a trail of devastation would be left by an Elizabeth Taylor if, along with her other attributes, she could also make the Boiled Dinner!

In the business world, what a sweeping up and

monopolizing of the nation's advertising accounts would result if the talents of a Mary Wells Lawrence were augmented by the reputation of being a Transcendental Boilist!

In Washington, what political power might be added to the charm and ability of a Margaret Chase Smith! With a mastery of the Boiled Dinner she might be able to take over the reins of government and establish a dictatorship which, while it would undoubtedly be benevolent under her, would expose the Republic to a dangerous precedent.

As the mind ranges over dozens of possibilities such as this, it must appear as the compensatory and somewhat concealed benefaction of a wise Providence (we must continually be on the lookout for blessings such as this or else we may not see them) that in the manufacture of the wondrous work that is Woman the ability to make the Transcendental Boiled Dinner has been in most cases deliberately left out.

8 ⟿ AN APPRENTICE APPEARS ·
HE IS PUT THROUGH A TRIAL
BOILING · HIS EXPERIENCES IL-
LUSTRATE COMMON FAILINGS ·
THE APPRENTICE CATECHIZED ·
HE MAKES A NEAR-FATAL BLUN-
DER FOLLOWED BY A SPLENDID
AND GRATIFYING RECOVERY · ·

THE Transcendental Boiled Dinner described in chapters 4, 5 and 6 was boiled near the end of June, 1970. The following summer, at the same time of that month, I was again at the old farm with various members of my family, and among these was the Nephew who had partaken of the Transcendental Boiled Dinner with me a year previously.

Having had a glimpse—or I should say, rather, a taste—of this gastronomical paradise, the Nephew asked if I would not conduct him through the procedure of cooking the Dinner, and when I agreed to do so, there occurred to him a further thought. This was that he might become the first member of a league or guild of Master Boiled Dinner Makers, who would serve apprenticeships and be certified and thus form an organization that would perpetuate the standards and ideals of the Boiled Dinner and convey its delights to future generations.

I was quick to point out the rather considerable difficulties entailed by this scheme. For example, suppose that the Master Boiler, even if certified, dwelt in Philadelphia. Would he be expected to boil the Dinner in waters drawn from the Schuylkill, chlorinating and otherwise chemicalizing the sweet carrots, tender cabbage and other wholesome ingredients in this witches' brew? The Nephew replied that if pure spring water were to be an essential requirement, it could be procured from commercial suppliers of such water. This exchange was fairly typical of several that followed in which I raised objections and my Nephew disposed of them with appropriate arguments, culminating in his saying that all great movements, as they have swept across the world, passing from one region and country to another, have always adapted themselves successfully to differing climates and customs.

I must say that at that moment I received a sudden and profound insight into how such movements get started. You see, it is not the nominal Founder at all who is responsible. It is that first disciple. Or perhaps the first four or five. It is they who organize and institutionalize. It is they who make rules and allow for dispensations. The spring water is a good example. Of course a commercial supplier can provide it. But will there be a speckled trout in his spring? And what about all the other influences of Nature of which I have spoken, many of them almost imperceptible, but all somehow mystically blending into a supernaturally delicious result?

It is this feeling for, this grasp of, the total concept that the Founder has and cannot pass on. Thus, although he may be given credit for the Movement, which may even be named after him, the Founder himself gradually recedes into the background.

Yet his writings, encapsulated in the Organization, preserved and re-consulted, will now and then give rise to a renaissance of true believers, and it is with this hope that I continue.

I am going to proceed now with the record of my Nephew's performance as an apprentice, and my critique of this performance, with the hope that the reader will learn from the practical difficulties which he experienced. Many of these are hardly to be expected, even from reading the voluminous and detailed instructions I have already given.

For example, I have mentioned the importance of absolute freedom from distraction, and I am sure the reader took note of this warning, and yet, like so many other warnings, it has failed in the absence of the actual circumstances presenting the hazard to impress itself sufficiently upon the mind. I have also mentioned, as a requisite for the character of the Master Boiler, the ability to take note of small signals of coming trouble—those tiny red flares no larger than a wink of the faintest star which sometimes flash in our consciousness only to go unheeded.

In the case of my Nephew's trial cooking, the first of his difficulties was heralded when his Aunt Ruth, after having been requested to stay out of the kitchen for the next four or five hours, entered and inquired if she might be allowed to make a blueberry pie. This would only take a few minutes and, once put into the oven, would be entirely out of the way, and there would be no interference whatever with the Boiled Dinner, we were assured. And indeed, this initially proved to be the case. She conducted herself quietly. The pie created no great commotion. We were relatively undisturbed. However, this was only a wedge. It next appeared that there was a basket of wet clothes in the kitchen which had been brought from the laundromat, and these had to be taken to the clothesline. And so with one thing and another she was in and out of the kitchen on several occasions, and on a few of these her original civility gave way to skeptical and even derisory remarks pertaining to the Boiled Dinner which, I thought, were far from being conducive to my Nephew's peace of mind or to his confidence in his preceptor. Once I thought I even heard the word "fanatic" in something she whispered to him.

With that necessary background, the trial boiling of

the Apprentice is best summarized by the actual work sheet and an explanation of the demerits entered upon it.

Demerits are indicated by asterisks (*) followed by numbers corresponding to the explanations.

The form will be recognized as that of the prescribed tables upon which the mathematics of the Boiled Dinner are worked out.

STANDARD TABLE		MODIFIED TABLE	ADJUSTED TABLE
Beef starts simmer	2:00 P.M.	2:34 P.M. *1 *2 *3	
Turnip insertion	5:16 P.M.	5:50 P.M. *4 *5	
Potato insertion	5:31 P.M.	6:05 P.M.	6:06 P.M.
Cabbage insertion	5:41 P.M.	6:15 P.M.	6:16 P.M.
Carrot insertion	5:46 P.M.	6:20 P.M.	6:21 P.M.
Dinner done	6:00 P.M.	6:34 P.M.	6:35 P.M.

The first thing that will be noticed (in the very first entry) is the great variance between the Standard and the Modified tables—34 minutes. This predicts a common failing on the part of beginning boilers; they will tend not to begin the Preliminary Boiling in time and so will wind up lagging far behind the Standard timetable. However, this does not necessarily call for a demerit. It is still within the bounds of acceptable procedure. Its only effect is to make those waiting for the Dinner hungrier than they might otherwise have been.

The real demerits incurred by the Apprentice were as follows:

1. *At 2:54 there occurred a serious lapse of monitoring. The Apprentice allowed the broth to boil vigorously for at least a minute. He offered as an excuse the fact that he had been called outside to help his Aunt Ruth with the clothesline. The excuse was not acceptable. I pointed out to him that the Master Boiler, in his determination to exclude all causes of distraction, including persons if necessary, must be absolutely implacable (I believe that in an attempt to season my criticism with a bit of kindly levity I did say "Ruthless" rather than "implacable"). I also observed to him that in going out to the clothesline he left the kitchen door open, and that although I myself was surprised at what happened to the Dinner, I could only surmise that leaving the door open had brought about a sudden change in the ambient atmosphere, stimulated rapid evaporation and caused a reduction of the volume of broth which, however slight, had been sufficient to set off the forbidden boiling.*

2. *At 3:25 occurred a failure in the opposite extreme—he allowed the simmering to subside and the broth to become placid for well over a minute.*

3. *In an excess of caution, possibly due to my having emphasized the necessity of having all vegetables in readiness prior to the beginning of the tension-filled last period of forty-five minutes, the Apprentice peeled the vegetables an hour and a half in advance and failed to*

submerge them entirely in cold water, until reminded to do so.

4. Turnip Error.

5. The Apprentice has failed to pay sufficient attention to, or make adequate record of, the nature and character of the day, which unfortunately has not been typical of this time of year. That is, instead of filling up with the usual cumulus clouds in the afternoon, the sky has now, at 6 P.M., opened up into an unbroken expanse of the deepest and clearest blue, a most unusual condition for late June. Thus, the procedure of a year ago has been somewhat unreliable as a guide. This "opening up" of the day may explain the eccentric behavior and sudden boiling of the broth which resulted in Demerit No. 1. However, the Apprentice should have been more alert and watchful, and if he had paid closer attention to all aspects of the day outside, comparing these with the record of a year ago, he might have been forewarned.

Although the dinner was not Transcendental in quality, it was acceptable and edible. Where it failed of perfection, I believe, was mainly in the last forty-five minutes, a period when, as I have repeatedly pointed out, the greatest mental poise, concentration and agility are required. In my Nephew's case, he became flustered and committed the dreaded Turnip Error, from which there is no possibility of recovery. The ultimate result was that he had to go light on the Cabbage—there was not enough room left for it in the pot when he got to Cabbage insertion—and this gave the dinner a little more of a turnipy flavor than it should have had. And, of course, a little less of a cabbagey.

It could not be said at this point that the Nephew had qualified as a Master Boiler. However, in view of the general level of competence he had displayed, and the extreme distractions that had beset him, I determined to evaluate his final prospects on an oral examination.

Our interview, after ranging over several aspects of the Boiled Dinner, finally came to a discussion of the character of the boiler.

We spoke of the desirability of a high rating on the Franklin–Edwards Scale.

Of the unsuitability of most women for this assignment.

Of alertness. Diligence. Devotion to duty.

And so forth.

Then, on what was apparently a sudden and ill-considered impulse—or perhaps it was merely a continuation of his organizing and institutionalizing trend of thought—my Nephew asked me if I thought the League of Master Boiled Dinner Makers, assuming that one came into existence, ought to have a code of ethics to subscribe to.

I could not have been more shocked if a thunderclap had sounded in the room.

Instantly, by his face, I could see that from looking at *my* face he realized that he had committed an unforgivable *faux pas*. I must have been livid with rage.

No thought he could possibly have had, once allowed to gain expression, could have betrayed a more thorough lack of understanding of the *ethic* (not a code of ethics) which underlies the whole spirit and concept of preparing the New England Boiled Dinner of Transcendental quality.

I suppose I must have subjected the poor boy, who was now half terrified at the obvious effects of his question, to a half hour's tirade, the substance of which is that when one sees a group of people of any sort subscribing to a code of ethics it can be adduced as certain that rascality is rampant among them, otherwise the code would not have been called for, and further, since the miscreants are by its publication certified as being in existence, the code will have no effect whatever unless it be disadvantageous to the public; the honest members will simply keep on being honest, which they would have done at any rate, while the rascals will use the code to perpetrate their rascality, as much further as it may be extended, upon their gullible victims.

No! I concluded, the convictions of the Master Boiler are not formed by looking at a printed card, posted on the wall. They are within him, inherent, unshakable and completely unsusceptible to external influences of any sort. They are between him and *his* Maker, only.

I then quoted one of the Resolutions which Jonathan Edwards wrote for his own guidance (a resolution for one's own guidance being quite different from an externally composed code of ethics). This was Edwards' Number 19: "Never do anything, which I should be afraid to do, if I expected it would not be above an hour, before I should hear the last trump."

That is your only ethic for the Master Boiler!

I had been so vehement in all this that I next endeavored to set the boy, who had perhaps been overalarmed and disquieted, at ease by a few jocular remarks, my intent also being to cause him to relax and let down his guard while he was being put to the next item of the catechism, the most important of all.

Thus, after a period of light conversation and a few questions of no great importance, I casually said, "Now it will naturally occur to many people, and may possibly occur to you, that there are other ingredients which would improve the quality of the Boiled Dinner. Let us consider one. Would you put in an onion?"

What was my rejoicing when he answered, No!

And with that I gave him the utmost encouragement that I would eventually certify him as a Master Boiler, conditional upon his correcting a few minor deficiencies that had been observed in his procedure. These did not matter. Neither did it matter that he could not fully explain why he would not add the onion. In fact, I was somewhat pleased that he could not, judging that his understanding rested upon an instinct too deep for articulation and therefore all the more impregnable.

What mattered was that he was sound in the faith!

He had struck error under the fifth rib!

And by that one blow he had redeemed himself!

In explanation of this, I now go on to the next chapter, which deals with heresy and the fundamental nature of sin in relation to the Boiled Dinner.

9 ❧ ANOTHER INFLAMMATORY SUBJECT RAISED · THE ONION AS AN INGREDIENT OF THE BOILED DINNER · ITS SINFUL AND DISRUPTIVE NATURE · THE READER WARNED AGAINST TEMPTATION · EXCOMMUNICATION PRONOUNCED UPON THE ONION · RECOMMENDED PENALTIES AND PUNISHMENTS FOR THOSE WHO WOULD PROFANE THE DINNER ·

N my remarks touching upon women in relation to the Boiled Dinner, I am aware that I may have aggrieved a few of them, yet I have proceeded with equanimity, knowing I could trust to the gracious and forgiving nature of womankind in general. Now, however, I venture out upon a subject that is certain to stir up unappeasable fires of indignation.

I have left this subject until toward the last not only to place it in the classic position of emphasis but because I have been sure all along that its introduction would arouse animadversion and contumacy of so violent a nature that any reasonable discussion would immediately terminate.

Now, however, since I believe I have deposited with the reader the essential body of information, exhortation and advice needed to prepare the Transcendental Boiled Dinner (or attempt to prepare it), I am ready to drive home the final point of doctrine without regard for the fact that it will arouse the clamor of the willful and wicked. Once having struck this blow for truth, I will then be content to make my bow and retire amidst the flames of controversy, serene in the realization that I have done my duty.

This chapter has to do with consideration of the onion as an ingredient of the Transcendental Boiled Dinner.

It will surely be remembered from Chapter 6 how earnestly I have emphasized the necessity of a theological point of view that will exclude from the Dinner *all* ingredients except those I have appointed as being fit and worthy.

To all these excluded things the onion stands as does Satan to his hosts of minor fiends, demons and evil spirits!

It is the apotheosis of all that is foreign and un-reconcilable to the Dinner—and of all that would sub-vert, corrupt and destroy it!

I once had a conversation with a lady whom under the circumstances I do not wish to identify, and it went about like this:

"Do you eat onions?"

"Yes," she replied.

"Don't they bother you?"

"Not much."

"Ah. Then they *do* bother you *some?*"

"Yes."

"Then why do you eat onions?"

"Because I love them—and I keep hoping I'll get away with it."

There, dear friends, is the perfect, the classic, de-lineation of SIN!

Of all the vegetables forbidden to the Transcen-dental Boiled Dinner, the onion is the most damaging yet the most seductive—the one most likely to suggest itself.

With all solemnity and certainty I warn the reader, even if he is the most upright of persons—one who would reject any thought of coveting the neighbor's wife, or the neighbor's ox, or of any other wrongdoing—that while he is striving for the Transcendental Boiled Dinner, this idea will creep temptingly into his mind: "Why not put in an onion?"

Heed not the voice of the Serpent!

It is here that the candidate for gastronomical paradise must hold unflinchingly to the principle of Infant Damnation.

It is here that he must recognize the onion for what it is: a child of wrath, predestined for eternal (and internal) torment . . . for "exquisite horrible misery"!*

Piquant and seductive though it may be, and swallowed with such guilty pleasure, nevertheless it remains unredeemed and unrepentant, giving rise to noxious vapors, disturbing the stomach and causing groans that cannot be uttered.

Moreover, its blasphemous and mischievous influence completely corrupts and destroys the sweet harmony of Beef bone, Turnip, Potato, Cabbage and Carrot, causing turbulence, disorder and uneasy passions where the most heavenly and joyful flavor was meant to reign.

Put an onion in a Boiled Dinner?

I would as soon add brimstone to its sweet and savory broth!

I am willing to admit that some of my best friends eat onions (although these are people I have watched closely for a reasonable length of time—say, ten or fifteen years—to make sure that this one failing did not signify the existence of other, and hidden, vices), and some dishes, I am willing to concede, possess sufficient strength of virtue so that onions may be added to them without so great a degree of harm.

But for him who enters upon the straight and narrow pathway that leads to the supreme bliss of the

* A phrase from that splendid sermon by Jonathan Edwards, "Sinners in the Hands of an Angry God."

Transcendental Boiled Dinner, there can be no compromise. He may possibly reach his goal—even by accident and good luck—if he forswears the onion.

But there is no way to get there *with* an onion.

Therefore, as a final point of doctrine addressed to my followers, I hereby excommunicate and anathematize this iniquitous vegetable and order it forever sequestered from the threshold of the Boiled Dinner.

And it is also declared that he who puts an onion into a New England Boiled Dinner should have his ears cropped, be whipped, branded on the forehead with the letter P (for Profaner) and made to stand in pillory.

I am aware that upon this point, more than on any other, clouds of disputants will arise to darken the air with false counsel and cries of indignation.

But let the aspiring maker of the Transcendental Boiled Dinner stand steadfast. Let him cast up his eyes to the patron saint of the Dinner, Jonathan Edwards, and hold firmly to that belief which is so essential to its preparation, the Doctrine of Original Sin!

10 ⤐ HAVING THOUGHT HE HAD CONCLUDED, THE AUTHOR IS NEVERTHELESS BESOUGHT TO CONTINUE · POSTPRANDIAL CONSIDERATIONS (AFTER THE BOILED DINNER, WHAT?) · THE READER IS COMFORTED AND CONSOLED BY WORDS OF TIMELY WISDOM · · · · · · ·

UPON concluding the previous chapter it had been my dearest wish to stop there and to retire to some quiet place where I would be safe from such few members of Women's Liberation who have been so unreasonable as to take umbrage at my remarks, and from agents of the onion interests, who are very powerful in this country.

However, I was remonstrated with by a gentleman of great conscience and perception who pointed out that I was morally obligated to continue and to deal with the problem of "what remains ahead of the reader in life once he has prepared and eaten a Transcendental Boiled Dinner.

"It could be argued," he said, "that if your book is going to enable some of your readers to prepare such a dinner you must then take it as part of your responsibility to help them deal with the consequences."

It is a rebuke to my humanity that I did not think of this myself.

It so happens that, as I begin to think about it now, it is the last day of summer, 1971, and I am at the old farm where the Transcendental Boiling took place in June, 1970, and where it was again attempted by my Nephew in June, 1971. The early part of this September was miserable; we were lashed by winds and drenched with rain. The skies have cleared now, but except for a few languid Indian Summer days there will not be much more warm weather. The barn swallows packed up, took baths (by diving down and skipping themselves across the surface of the pond) and departed on September 8 or 9, a day or so early. Now as I look out past the old barn with its great open door from which they swooped so often, the sky is empty, and against it I notice another sign of autumn: a patch of blazing red in the top of the big spruce that stands behind the old granary. It is the only spruce tree I know that acts like a maple, but this, of course, is an illusion. A woodbine has wound its way to the top of the tree; its green leaves are invisible against the spruce boughs in summer but change to scarlet in the fall. Although not high for a spruce, the tree is enormous in girth—and is almost pyramidal in profile. It has grown out of a mulch of decaying sawdust where an icehouse once stood and provided for refrigeration (with ice we cut ourselves) in the days when this was an organic (organic was all we had), independent, self-sufficient, one-family farm. The spruce growing out of the sawdust pile somehow reminds me that this way of life, which has come to seem so desirable to many of the young people of today, has probably vanished forever in spite of their back-to-the-land efforts to revive it.

Just before dark I walked out to see whether the new moon had appeared and saw, instead, another sight that had a melancholy tinge. The sky in its everchanging sunset hues was at that moment a salmon pink, and against this background two jet planes had crossed at such an angle that their white trails had made a large X; it was as though they had X'ed out summer.

Then, Carrie came for supper, and she said that the Seven-Day Pickles are not up to par this fall because of a decline in the quality of the cider vinegar that is available in the stores; it is too strong. This does not present an insuperable problem. There is an old but still workable press on the premises and some trees in the orchard still bearing apples, and my brother the engineer, who is an accomplished ciderist, can make Carrie some vinegar of the required quality.

What is more disturbing is the fact that some of the ladies around here, including a couple near and dear to Carrie and me, are making what they call a Six-Day Pickle and have even been heard to say that it is "just as good as the Seven-Day." This is symbolic of what is wrong with our society today.

Perhaps these impressions, all of them autumnal in tone, influenced me in the advice I am now about to give the preparer or eater of the Transcendental Boiled Dinner as to what life holds for him subsequently.

I have concluded, first of all, that it would be fatuous to use the Boiled Dinner as a means of exhortation toward continued endeavor and higher achievements. The onward-and-upward, "a man's reach should exceed his grasp," keep-striving-for-perfection sort of thing is simply nonsense. The Transcendental Dinner, you see, may be a single occurrence. Even I am reconciled to the fact that I may never achieve one again.

In this light we now begin to see that our greatest lesson is not to be found in the Dinner itself, but in its afterglow.

For years the American expectation and dream has been of progress! success! victories! expansion! ever-increasing abundance! But now we are beginning to see there is another side to life. We have lost our first war. The environment, we are told, is collapsing. Inflation is on the way to putting most of us below the poverty level. The Yankees are finishing twenty games behind. And so on.

Furthermore, many of our young people have renounced the progress-success idea of life; and even those who have not, ironically enough, face a limited future. That is to say, with the emphasis on youth that exists in so many of our corporations and other activities (which strikes one as being the worst possible thing for young people), at the age of twenty-two, when most people are getting out of college, they can now look ahead to only fifteen or twenty years or so of productive life. How discouraging that will be, unless some sort of moral sustenance, some change of philosophy, comes to their aid!

It is with relation to this state that we all are in, the younger and the older, poor strugglers that we are, that the Boiled Dinner speaks to us. It reminds us that we need very little courage when we are climbing upward toward a sky that is bright with promise, and even less when we stand at the peak; it is when we level off and go downward, temporarily or permanently, that we must learn to take satisfaction in an ability to look realities in the face with a grim and unflinching stare. One thinks of Robert E. Lee, some time after Appomattox, asked by a mother how she should instruct her child and saying, "Teach him he must deny himself."

And to those whose attainments have been, are or promise to be exceptionally great, the message of the Boiled Dinner is even more explicit. It is that the greater the achievement, the likelier it is only to happen once. And after that, in that particular endeavor, it is all down grade.

Thus it could be with us who have known the Transcendental Boiled Dinner. We may be exactly in the case of the fellow who, seated one day at the organ, touched a chord that was "like the sound of a great

Amen." And that was it. He never found it again. It became the Lost Chord. But did the fellow give up music? We hope not. For there are other chords to be sounded and—who knows?—the sun may also occasionally shine on the other side of the hill.